PENGUINS

AND OTHER SEABIRDS

PENGUINS

AND OTHER SEABIRDS

MATT SEWELL

TEN SPEED PRESS

Berkeley

In loving memory of Pat Lee

Foreword by Brian Briggs 9

Introduction 11

Emperor Penguin 14

King Penguin 16

Brown Skua 19

Wandering Albatross 21

Storm Petrel 22

Northern Giant Petrel 24

Sooty Shearwater 27

Adélie Penguin 28

Gentoo Penguin 30

Striated Caracara 33

Snowy Sheathbill 34

Imperial Shag 36

Arctic Tern 39

Chinstrap Penguin 40

Northern and Southern
Rockhopper Penguin 42

Common Loon 45

Northern Fulmar 47

Parasitic Jaeger 48

Steller's Eider 50

King Eider 52

Macaroni Penguin 55

Royal Penguin 57

Harlequin Duck 58

Smew 60

Crested Auklet 63

Dovekie 65

Fiordland Crested
and Snares Penguin 66

Erect-crested Penguin 68

Great Auk 71

Razorbill 73

Guillemot 75

Puffin 76

Humboldt Penguin 78

African Penguin 81

Tufted Puffin 82

Rhinoceros Auklet 84

Great Cormorant 87

Gannet 88

Magellanic and
Galápagos Penguin 90

Little Penguin 92

Blue-footed Booby 95

Australian Pelican 97

Magnificent Frigatebird 98

Black Skimmer 100

Yellow-eyed Penguin 102

Surf Scoter 105

Osprey 107

White-tailed Sea Eagle 109

White-flippered Penguin 110

Gyrfalcon 112

Spotting and Jotting 114

Acknowledgments 128

FOREWORD

Seabirds inhabit the planet's greatest wilderness, and thinking of them out there now, in that vast, ever-changing landscape, fires the imagination like nothing else.

My personal favorite is the gannet—a distant, brilliant white cross, haunting the open seas from high above the waves, until it falls as though shot down, dislocating its wings as it moves between worlds of air and water.

Sadly, the imagination is as close as most of us can get to experiencing their world, but that distance is what makes them so inspiring to me. Fortunately, Matt's book of beautiful, distinctive interpretations of their sleek wind-shaped forms will have your mind soaring before you know it ...

Brian Briggs, frontman of Stornoway
and orinthologist

INTRODUCTION

When I first started researching this book, Google accidentally auto-suggested the question: "Are penguins fish or birds?" I spat my tea out laughing! But for the search engine to do that, a lot of people must have asked that very question. And penguins are pretty mysterious: cute, but actually very odd and distinct in their own way.

Mankind has always ascribed seabirds with a certain mystical quality, owing to their prowess in the air, their ease in and on water, their migrational comings and goings, and their sheer volume. They are souls of lost sailors, saints, storm-bringers, omens, witches, and warriors. They are also easy to catch, at risk from man-made as well as natural disasters ... no wonder many are endangered.

Hopefully in this book you will discover that there is a lot more to penguins than being cute. In fact, they are one of the hardiest souls on the planet, evolving millions of years ago to thrive in some of Earth's toughest and loneliest environments.

And they are definitely not fish!

THE BIRDS

Emperor Penguin
Aptenodytes forsteri

As penguins go, this guy is the boss, the sultan of the Antarctic snow. He's the star of Hollywood movies and blue-chip nature documentaries, so high and mighty among his penguin peers that he alone was chosen to represent his species on the wrapper of my favorite chocolate cookie. In his Olympic wetsuit, with eyes darker than Ozzy Osbourne's Ray-Bans, the Emperor is the biggest and heaviest of all known penguins—weighing the same as a fat Labrador retriever and standing just as tall as the dog on its back legs. His bulk isn't gained through being lazy; it comes from his "thermal underwear," a physical necessity to protect him and his offspring from the subzero temperatures of the South Pole as he and his Empress make babies during the winter. The females leave to recuperate after laying their eggs, feeding solo in the ocean while the males, for months, suffer the banshee-wailing whipping wind, snow drifts, and sunless gloom of new fatherhood. With temperatures at -94°F the daddies bunch together in a hundred-strong, rotating huddle, eggs safely tucked up on their shuffling feet inside the warm incubating brood pouch. Soon after the fluffy chicks hatch, the females return from the sea, fat, sleek, and healthy. They relieve the dad of his duties and—like ships that pass in the night—the Emperors slip off to feed themselves on fathoms-deep dives, reaching depths of 1,770 feet and holding their breath for 15 minutes at a time. Wow!

King Penguin
Aptenodytes patagonicus

Second to the Emperor, but still a King, our only other *Aptenodytes* family member stands 3 feet tall with a haughty air in his mithril silver cloak and glowing imperial topaz neckwear. His vivid opulence is a stark contrast to the rocky, snow-flecked terrain of the King Penguin's kingdom, which stretches from subantarctic islands, the Falklands and South Georgia, to parts of Australia and even as far north as Argentina. Living in more hospitable conditions than the Emperors, the Kings share the parental day-to-day duties of caring for their egg and, eventually, their chick, which—especially when compared to the dignified nobility of its folks—looks like an awkward toddler in a Sasquatch outfit. These baby Bigfoots gang up and hang out, forming crèches in defense against the predatory skuas and Giant Petrels while their folks are off feeding and stocking up in the ocean, expertly avoiding killer whales and leopard seals. Despite these everyday struggles and the fact that they were once massively hunted for food, fuel, and their warm feathery robes, the King Penguins' population is figured to be well over a whopping 2 million pairs.

Brown Skua
Catharacta antarctica

The shadow that hangs above our penguins.
Eggs, chicks, and even adult birds are never safe
from the largest and heaviest skua's murderous
threat. In their dark domain the whole world
is their enemy, and perhaps their prey, too.
Colonizing wherever you find penguins, from
the Antarctic up to Chile, their story of life and
survival has played on repeat for millions of
years, and hopefully it will run for millions more.

Wandering Albatross
Diomedea exulans

The slow arcing flight of an albatross,
considered and interminable like a glacier,
is a radiant rhapsody to behold. His solitary,
athletic glide embraces every faint breath
of wind to propel him forever onward, taut
and muscular like the sails of a clipper ship.
Hundreds of nautical miles are swept away on
one wingbeat of a wingspan of over 10 feet. The
exiled Wandering Albatross of the Southern
Ocean, with his lovebite and prominent brow,
has the largest wingspan of any living bird.
Landing only to breed after charming courtship
"sky pointing" dances, the albatross returns
to the air, living over 50 years and clocking up
millions of carbon-free miles. If only all air
travel could be as clean as that achieved by this
magnificent bird of good omen.

Storm Petrel
Oceanites oceanicus

No bigger than the finches, sparrows, and chickadees that you find in your garden, these small cabin boys are actually very able ancient mariners, spending the majority of the year out at sea in all weather—rain or shine. Superstitious sailors believed they foretold stormy weather and imagined them as souls of dead seamen as they followed batlike in their wake. During particularly inclement times they can be blown far inland, giving them their name: Storm Petrel. The seabird's fluttery leg-dangling flight has also given rise to the name of a whole host of his relatives as well; "Petrel" is inspired by the way the feeding bird looks like he is walking on water, just like St. Peter did on the Lake of Galilee. The family include Prions, Gadflies, and Diving Petrels, plus many others, including the Black-Caped Petrel, which was recently rediscovered after 150 years. They can be found in every sea in the world, but the Storm Petrel in particular can be found off the west coast of the UK, and the Wilson's Petrel with the Gentoo Penguins on the Antarctic coasts.

Northern Giant Petrel
Macronectes halli

Hell's seagull! It's hard to understand how
this carrion-loving, offal-devouring bulkhead
can be related to the bewitching Storm Petrel—
but he is, and it's all in the family nose. Like
shearwaters, fulmars, and all the other petrels of
the world, Northern Giant Petrels have plated
beaks with tubular noses. These prominent
nostrils are used to expel excessive salt from the
constant barrage of briny seawater taken in by
the glands above the eye that act as secondary
kidneys. Apparently they aid smell, too,
helping the Northern Giant Petrel sniff out his
next ill-begotten death-rolled meal.

Sooty Shearwater
Ardenna grisea

In the UK there are the enigmatic Manx Shearwaters of the Isle of Man and across Europe there are a handful of relatives, including the Balearic Shearwater, which heralds from the party islands of the Mediterranean. No celebrations here, though, as tough action is being taken to up the bird's status on the critically endangered list. The life of the tall, dark, and handsome Sooty Shearwater most definitely deserves an honorable mention, however. These long-distance mariner migrants undertake an epic voyage after rearing their sooty chicks in their breeding colonies on the cliffs of New Zealand, Chile, Australia, and the Falkland Islands. Setting out to sea on their bladelike wings that shear the water's surface, the subantarctic Sooty Shearwaters set sail on an adventure that takes them on a clockwise circular journey up the western side of the Pacific, across the subarctic paleocrystic seas, and back down the eastern side of the oceans to a welcome-home party in honor of these legendary globe-trotting travelers.

Adélie Penguin
Pygoscelis adeliae

These are good-time penguins who, for flightless birds, handily excel at getting about on dry but icy land. They have the trademark wobbling waddle of penguins, but are surprisingly fast and very capable long-distance walkers in their oversize rented tuxedos. Living alongside the Emperor Penguins on the permafrosted floes of the Antarctic coastline, the Adélies follow the sun as it mutes in tone and drops ever deeper on the horizon, ice thickening with its slow edging creep. All penguins are insulated with a puffer-jacket effect—the skin has two layers, one of blubber and the other of feathers; the latter also has two layers, one stiff, the other downy, trapping warm air inside—and the Adélies also style out the winter season in this way. Optimistically remaining in the light and by the sea, the troupes raise their young in stone-lined nests, feeding them from fishing trips that can last as long as 3 days at sea. The Adélie Penguins' name comes from the sweetheart of a Napoleonic naval captain turned explorer, who claimed for France an area of the Antarctic where the penguins were first recorded. He christened the lands and the birds after the love of his life: his wife Adélie.

Gentoo Penguin
Pygoscelis papua

A member of the Brush-tailed family, this penguin is awarded the title Penguin with the Longest Tail (we are not talking peacock tail–long here, but in the subtly different world of the penguins, anything a tiny bit different is deemed a distinguishing feature and worth celebrating). Alongside his long tail, the Gentoo can be spotted and jotted by the white patches above his eyes, which look as though the black enamel he was painted with has been chipped off. He can swim so fast that he would get a ticket in a pedestrian zone—and he also has a thing for stones. The circular nests of the Gentoo rookeries are lined with prized pebbles and guarded like the crown jewels. Bungled heists by butterfingered rubble robbers are everyday plot lines played out in the colonies of these penguins and, once purloined, these precious crystals are lovingly presented to the females, strengthening their bond. Maybe that is where the Gentoo derive their name—their gentlemanly gifts. (Let's just ignore the fact that they're actually stolen goods.)

Striated Caracara
Phalcoboenus australis

Caracaras are a family of forest falcons established along the whole of South and Central America. They are long-limbed hawklike birds; the handsome Southern Crested Caracara is a particular favorite of mine. The Striated Caracara, whose name was given due to his "straight," gray, steel-like chest feathers, is the southernmost and only typical bird of prey of the subantarctic region. Not a typical falcon that takes quarry in flight, however: he is a scavenger, a chancer, and like the crow, kea, and gray parrot, a highly intelligent bird who would rather use his wit over his wings. Known as Johnny Rook on the Falkland Islands—and persecuted there due to a penchant for newborn lambs—he is famous for stealing red objects and anything that a peer is carrying. Caracaras also have a thing for Rockhopper Penguin chicks, and that breeding season is bountiful for the Striated Caracara; after that, he is back to his usual resourceful and mischievous ways.

Snowy Sheathbill
Chionis albus

This is a really weird bird that looks part
seagull but without the webbed feet, pigeonlike
in shape but with turkey-esque wattles, and
with a cutthroat dagger for a beak.
But Snowy Sheathbills are actually most
closely related to mudlarking waders. They
must be very hardy, as they are the only
birds endemic to Antarctica as well as its
surrounding islands. Like all the non-seabirds
of this harsh terrain, they are resourceful,
omnivorous, and brave. They steal penguins'
eggs and even the food out of the chicks'
mouths; their small size does not make them
any less fearless. You can't help but feel for the
penguins, though: when they are not getting
stalked in the sea by leopard seals and orcas,
or bracing themselves for death from above
by skuas and Giant Petrels, they are getting
mugged on foot by weird snowy pigeons.

Imperial Shag
Phalacrocorax atriceps

This common seabird of the Southern Ocean
is also known as Antarctic Shag and the
King Cormorant—the noble moniker is easy
to understand when the Blue-eyed shag is
compared to the humble shag of the Great
British coastline. He is, of course, a great spot
on any given day ... but I am truly fascinated
by the Imperial Shag's amazing azure-blue
eye ring and the yellow knob on the beak,
which looks like a big blob of pollen on a
bumble bee's leg. And don't forget that quiff of
feathers! But put them all together and I have
to admit his name is maybe too highborn; for as
courtly as he is, I can't help but be reminded of
a medieval jester. When he is rubbing shoulders
with King Penguins, he might be just that.

Arctic Tern
Sterna paradisaea

The Sea Swallow (as one might term the Arctic Tern) could easily be the most graceful bird of the ocean, who, like his fork-tailed far-flying compatriot on dry land, takes on a herculean annual trans-equatorial migration. Dove white, with crystal-gray wings, a fine beak, and legs of beaming buoy-red, the Arctic Tern is as clean-cut and stylish on the ground as he is in the air. Every day is a holiday for these sun-worshipping sightseers who have two summers a year. They have to work for it, though, breeding in great numbers during the spring and summer months in Norfolk, England and upward from there, along either side of the Atlantic and Pacific Oceans, all the way to the most northern point of Greenland. Then the change comes: there are subtle drops in temperature and the Arctic Tern starts to feel a pinch of *Zugunruhe*—getting itchy feet. Plans are made for the birds' circumpolar vacation and the course is set for Antarctica via the coast of Africa and then back again via South America—which is only a journey of 4,000 miles! Incredible. And to think they make this pilgrimage every year—and can live to over thirty! A seabird that weighs the same as a small bag of candy can fly to the moon and back three times in its lifetime ... now, that's hard to swallow!

Chinstrap Penguin
Pygoscelis antarctica

This brilliantly named bird really does look like he is wearing a shiny black skullcap helmet with a tight-fastening chinstrap—perfect to keep it in place on the daring feeding runs, glancing off lunges from orcas. All penguins have evolved to be supreme swimmers. Normally, birds have hollow bones for lightness in flight, but penguins have solid, heavier bones that help with buoyancy. Although thought to be brown originally, penguins ingeniously evolved through time to be pied. With their white bellies being a defense against the predators that stalk them from below, making them look like bright surface daylight, and their backs being black from above, camouflaging with the sea to prevent aerial attacks, this cunning machination is called "countershading." The darkness of penguins' eyes helps them adapt from the brightness of their snow-covered surroundings to their murky underwater hunts, with an added third eyelid offering extra protection during the speed of the chase. These amazing facts all prove that the penguin may appear clumsy but has evolved to become one of the best-equipped birds in the word.

Northern and Southern Rockhopper Penguin
Eudyptes moseleyi and *Eudyptes chrysocome*

Rocking up as they do at almost 20 inches tall, these guys are the pocket-size rock stars of the bird world: leather-clad Heavy Metalers in black denim and cheap eyeliner, with wet-look gel spikes on top and a bleached-blonde shoulder-length mullet at the back. It's not their headbanging that made their name, though: it's their agility on terra firma considering the fact that most penguins prefer to slide like a toboggan on their tummies or climb clumsily. In contrast, our hero here prefers to jump, dive, and hop from morning to bedrock. The Rockhoppers come in two different species but look near enough exactly the same: the Northern gang lives in large colonies in New Zealand and also in the Indian Ocean, while the Southern posse roams off Chile, Argentina, and the Falklands. They are the stars of many a kids' animated film, but both species conservationally are under threat, with populations dropping dangerously since the 1950s due to oil spills, overfishing, and climate change.

Common Loon
Gavia immer

The diver family, including the Black-throated
and the striking Red-throated Diver, are
devilishly handsome seabirds of Admiralty
class and are prodigious and polished predators
of fish and mollusks in the shallow waters and
sheltered bays of Western Europe, Canada,
and North America. Also known as Great
Northern Divers, Common Loons breed in the
summer months in the US's Great Lakes and
reservoirs, and their calls are as much a part of
that environment as mallard quacks and goose
honks are to those in the UK. The spooky
yodeling call of the loon can be heard echoing
over the bayou and is the characteristic that
gives the bird its name. I've never heard them
in situ but personally I don't think the name is
that apt for such beautiful, deep-black-green
birds with expressive calligraphic markings,
not to mention their talent, dexterity, and
bravery while out in the dark briny waters.

Northern Fulmar
Fulmarus glacialis

If it weren't for the Fulmars' tube-nose, they
would be easily mistaken for a common gull;
they are stocky and strong but sweet like a
minivan and found everywhere—from the Arctic
Circle, along the summer coasts of Britain, and
all the way to Asia. These once rare look-alikes
were for a time found exclusively on the now
uninhabited Scottish archipelago of St. Kilda,
where they were hunted for a motley collection
of uses—food, down for pillows, oil for lamps,
and medicine. Luckily, the Fulmars were not
overhunted and their populations are looking
safe, but still approach with caution as these
passive-aggressive gulls defensively spray any
approaching personage, be they friend or foe,
with a jet of rancid-smelling oil from the pits of
their stomachs. A gush of gull guts to the face is
not a good way to start the day.

Parasitic Jaeger
Stercorarius parasiticus

These birds come in various shades and morphs, but always have two long tail feathers that look like a couple of fish have taken a bite to hitch a ride, train-surfer style. A very common seabird in the cold tundras of North America and Eurasia, they can be spotted in Scotland during the breeding season in summer and also around the UK coast throughout the migrational phase in autumn, that going-back-to-school time. In the UK they are known as the Arctic Skua, but I much prefer its alternate denomination of Parasitic Jaeger, as it is a precise narration of this bully bird's tyrannizing tactics. All skuas are well known for their pursuing, piratical behavior and their kleptoparasitism, but these guys have taken it to a new level, specializing in the unceasing robbing of gulls and charming terns. To have the moves like a Jaeger you just have to chase, harangue, and bully somebody until he drops his lunch. Jaegers just need to chill out a bit and go and pick on someone their own size.

Steller's Eider
Polysticta stelleri

Steller's coat is imbued with deep hues of
cinnamon and enriched with Hubble Space–
telescopically deep navy-blue colors and
delicate details that seem more commonplace
on an ornate coral fish of the South Pacific
than on a hardy sea duck of the bitter north.
Breeding in Scandinavia, Japan, North America,
and Russia, the Eiders' populations have been
dropping, in particular in their historical
hometowns in Alaska. Let us hope it's not
because they make a handsome trophy for the
camouflaged duck hunters in their midst.

King Eider
Somateria spectabilis

It doesn't take a rocket scientist to work out
why this guy is known as the King of the
Eiders. He's big, one of the fastest birds in the
world, and his crowning vivid yellow coronet
is ensconced in light pastel tones and offset
with deep inky black delineations. His Latin
name means "remarkable" and "worth seeing."
I love the idea of white-bearded dudes in robes
packing their binoculars, a flask of tea, and
some cookies, and then heading out to spot a
Somateria spectabilis. He's a real ice-breaker,
but not just for his looks. In the summer, he
heads in the opposite direction as everybody
else and sets course for the desolate plains of the
Arctic to breed. You're going the wrong way!

Macaroni Penguin
Eudyptes chrysolophus

Our friend here doesn't beget this outlandish
moniker because sailors thought he tasted
good with a bowl full of pasta; if that were the
case, surely there wouldn't be any left, such is
man's greed. No: this fine-crested specimen
was likened to a peculiar posh gentleman's
fashion from the mid-eighteenth century.
Macaronis wore fancy clothes, sported huge,
ceiling-scraping wigs, and spoke their own
Latin slang—a precursor to the cocky New
Romantics of the 1980s. I personally think
it's rather harsh on the penguins; they may
be a bit dandy but they look like good, solid,
salt-of-the-earth types to me. The à la mode
Macaronis can be found on the same islands
of the Southern Ocean as the Southern
Rockhoppers and are also in decline—but
hopefully they will never go out of fashion.

Royal Penguin
Eudyptes schlegeli

May I present His Royal Highness of the Isle
of Macquarie? A brightly faced, gregarious,
banqueting medieval prince: good-humored
and good to his people. Not related to the other
noblemen—the Emperor and the King—our
aristocrat here is very much part of the Crested
Penguin lineage, but stands alone with his
white face and chin. Spending much of their
life in open sea, these royal birds alight on
rocky shores after feeding on krill and squid.
They breed only on one particular island in the
unforgiving waters between New Zealand and
Antartica: Macquarie Island. Penguins evolved
to live in the southern hemisphere only because
there were no land predators; you never see a
polar bear snacking on a penguin, do you? But
this localism is now a threat; whole species of
birds could be wiped out so easily it is scary.

Harlequin Duck
Histrionicus histrionicus

Found off coastlines in Greenland, Iceland,
North America, and Japan, the Harlequin
Ducks breed inland on fast-flowing rivers,
dabbling and bobbing like dinghies, and then
move out past the estuaries and river mouths
to the rocky shores to feed and spend the rest
of the year. They are known by many names
including Blue Streaks, Lords and Ladies,
and Painted Ducks, which allude to the birds'
distinct design of rusted red flanks and metallic
blue-and-white patches that look like reflected
light on calm water. It's a complex plumage
that chimes nicely with the mosaic-checkered
costumes of sixteenth-century harlequins.

Smew
Mergellus albellus

———————

Want to know why the Smew is my favorite
seabird, even though it's not actually that much
of a seabird, as seabirds go? It has the best name:
Smew. So cute. They look great; their cracked-ice
design is totally cool. And I just love the fact that
they spend most of the year in the wilderness on
oxbow lakes or by flooded forests, where they
nest in holes in broad-leaved trees way up in
the Balkans and over into Russia. When winter
arrives, they pull up stakes for warmer water,
many choosing estuaries, sheltered coastal bays,
and brackish lagoons around the North Sea to fish
and fatten up, while some can also be found on
UK winter lakes and reservoirs, also popular with
many visiting winter guests. Which is the best
thing, really—I can be in London on business,
wrapped up against the cold, visiting one of the
capital's many brilliant parks, and, if I am lucky, I
can spot and jot a Smew. It's got a lot going for it.

Crested Auklet
Aethia cristatella

The Crested Auklet looks completely
ridiculous and smells a little bit like Christmas.
It's true—and it's all to impress the ladies.
What with the birds' plumage that comes in
five shades of gray topped with an effervescent
perky crest, their trumpetlike flirtatious calls,
and their fabulously fragrant citrus cologne,
the Crested Auklet breeding season—on the
volcanic islands in the Sea of Okhotsk, in the
Bering Sea, and on the cliffs of Alaska—must
be like a nightclub on a Saturday evening.
Amazingly, the males during this time emit
a strong scent that is strikingly similar to
tangerines—a smell that will always remind me
of childhood yuletides. I hope I find a Crested
Auklet in my Christmas stocking this year!

Dovekie
Alle alle

Also known as the Little Auk, the Dovekie has a really sweet, dovelike quality. He easily gives the Puffin a run for his money in the cuteness stakes, while actually being only half his size— that being similar to the dimensions of a starling, but much fatter (but please don't tell him that!). Dovekies are just as sociable as starlings, too. As the communal starling does, they muster together in great flocks—and when they are not at roost on high, wave-battered cliffs, they are out at sea together en masse: safety in numbers. They winter off the coasts of Canada, North America, Scandinavia, and the UK, coming down from their subarctic frozen nesting sites to find their new abodes. Gusty squalls have been known to push rafts of the Dovekies inland— what an amazing sight that would be.

Fiordland Crested and Snares Penguin
Eudyptes pachyrhynchus and *Eudyptes robustus*

These aren't penguins of the fjordlands of Norway; unfortunately, there aren't many penguins north of the equator. Although, in the 1930s, a tiny raft of King Penguins was introduced to a small, predator-free island in northern Norway ... but sadly it didn't take off, which is strange for flightless birds. The lands in question here are the New Zealand locations of the Fiordland Crested Penguin and Snares Penguin, which are pretty much the same bird except for their hometowns and a tiny bit of bare skin under the Snare's beak to spot the difference, but we won't split hairs here.

Erect-crested Penguin
Eudyptes sclateri

Another Crested Penguin from New Zealand—
our friend here has a very fine and jaunty display
with which to impress the lady penguins and
also face down love rivals. At 18 inches tall, they
are the biggest out of the crested cousins, but
alike in that they don't have the widest spread
of populations, once again choosing to inhabit
mostly one small island off the coast of Australia
and New Zealand. These homes of the Crested
Penguins were once predator-free—apart from
the omnipresent shadow of the skuas—but
accidentally introduced animals are now slowly
decimating their numbers. It defies reason that a
bird that stands at 18 inches tall and weighs the
same as a very fat cat can be critically endangered
by a rodent that from nose to tail is 3 inches
long and punches in at the same weight as a blue
chickadee. Sadly, with our help, house mice have
made voyage to these archipelagos … and have
discovered a liking for penguin eggs.

Great Auk
Pinguinus impennis

The story of the Great Auk is a miserable maritime tragedy. Once, millions of these large seabirds could be found roosting, paired for life, on the coastlines of Western Europe, North America, and Canada ... and now they are all gone. Hunted for oil, feathers, and flesh, the clumsy bird was easy pickings, especially for starving sailors who would herd whole islands of birds onto their ships. The Great Auk is the original penguin (*Pinguinus*), though the two aren't related; our Antarctican friends found their name after being mistaken for the Auk, who was just as agile and graceful in the water but ever so cumbersome and awkward on dry land. Extinct since 1840, the very last Great Auk was caught and stoned to death; it was believed to be a witch, such was its strange looming presence coming out of the water (Great Auks were about 30 inches tall). With the fatal blow, its whole species was condemned to mythology.

Razorbill
Alca torda

———————

Chunky like a tugboat, the bullfinch of the sea
world has a tungsten-tough, shiny black beak,
which looks perfect for shucking oysters, although
the Razorbill has more of a liking for tiny krill.
Using their wings to fly through the sea, all auks,
this one included, are amazing swimmers and the
tiniest crustacean prey is the easiest of dinners
for these North Atlantic brawny bathers.

Guillemot
Uria aalge

The humble Guillemot, also known as the
Common Murre, is a family member of the
Auks, along with the Puffin, the Razorbill, and
others. They are one of the UK's most common
coastal birds, but live out of reach on white
painted cliffs in seabird cities—still an amazing
spot if you get the chance. They are easily
mistaken for oil-slicked penguins when they
are washed up far away from home on tourists'
beaches, even if you know what you're looking
for. They can dive as deep as 600 feet; they must
keep their fish sticks in Davy Jones' Locker.

Puffin
Fratercula arctica

Found on grassy offshore escarpments on both sides of the Atlantic, Puffins are usually running around like face-painted puppies at a seaside birthday party. The sea parrot's vivid, fascinating beak is not for crunching through crusty crabs; it's for carrying home their catch of the day, and it can hold up to ten fish at one time. (It also comes in very handy for dazzling the female Puffins.) Nesting in burrows and rocky holes, Puffins live in great colonies; there are outposts of over a million birds in some parts of Iceland. After the breeding season, they head out to open water and spend the winter at sea. A popular bird of culture and found on many a card and calendar, the Puffin's large population—which was once overhunted and affected by our overfishing—is now believed to be safe. But on the UK's fair isles, rocks that were once abundant with the gregarious seabirds are falling quiet. Hopefully they will come flocking home again soon.

Humboldt Penguin
Spheniscus humboldti

Although all Banded Penguins look very similar,
out of this group the Humboldt may be the most
familiar to many readers. A famous mainstay
at the London Zoo from as far back as the
1930s, the Humboldts were originally housed
in the ultra-Modernist penguin pool designed
by pioneering architect Berthold Lubetkin;
it's an amazing building but one not entirely
sympathetic to the penguins' needs nor their
usual habitat of their South American homelands
along the coastline of Peru and Chile, off the
upswelling Humboldt current. And in the 1930s,
a designer of a fledgling publishing house spent
the day at the London Zoo studying the birds
to create a logo for the company. You probably
have one of its offerings on your bookshelf. As
stylized as it is, the Penguin Books logo is very
much a Humboldt Penguin.

African Penguin
Spheniscus demersus

Many a penguin has washed up onto the shores of the diverse and remarkable African continent, but our friend here is the only penguin truly endemic to Africa. Known locally as the Black-Footed or Cape Penguin, it is actually found in a much wider geographical scope than just the Cape of Good Hope, reaching from Mozambique across the whole of South Africa's coastline, through to Namibia and into Angola. They have been a successful bird, suited to the cold Benguela Current, but populations have been dropping for many years due to local egg collection for food, overfishing, and oil pollution. Banded Penguins prefer a warmer climate, so they have never been found in the Antarctic. The naked pink patches on their faces are used to thermoregulate and cool down, and they are much less fatty compared to most other thermal-layered penguins. But a home in the sun comes with conditions attached, as it has the added threat of land-based predators to contend with. African Penguins prefer to keep to rocky islands, but they will always be in danger from mongooses, snakes, owls, and even leopards!

Tufted Puffin
Fratercula cirrhata

The Tufted Puffin lives on the other side of
the world to the Puffins we all know and love
so well, calling either side of the North Pacific
home, from California to Alaska and East Asia
through to Russia. Here they stand on the rock
face, breakers crashing around them, staring
out to the horizon with their fetlocks blowing
on the seaward breeze and their scintillating
beaks glowing in the briny spray. Handsome
chaps, aren't they? But both sexes look similar.
Much like the lavishly adorned Horned Puffin
of the same coastline, the Tufted Puffin is
much bigger than regular Puffins and every bit
the expert submariner and fisherman, too.

Rhinoceros Auklet
Cerorhinca monocerata

Our North Pacific–dwelling, be-horned seafaring friend is also known as the Unicorn Puffin—and it's easy to see why. That rhino horn is not used for skewering sailfish or for charging down film crews in Jeeps; rather, as with all the other auks with appendages, it's primarily noticed during breeding season, which is when this unicorn-like magic horn— along with fine tendril whiskers and shocks of Bride of Frankenstein eyebrows—is taken into consideration among the Auklet's peers. Whoever has the best gets the girl.

Great Cormorant
Phalacrocorax carbo

The fisherman's nemesis. The coastal bird
moves upstream during the summer for
pescatarian banquets and then, once gorged,
dries his pitch-dark wings like a riverbank
diabolo, scaring the anglers away. Cormorants
are found everywhere in the world except South
America and the polar regions. Although really
a coastal bird rather than an open-water seabird,
cormorants have also adapted to every kind
of waterway imaginable: deltas and estuaries,
mangrove swamps, marshes, lakes, reservoirs,
and huge meandering free-flowing rivers. The
Great Cormorant hails from a vast extended
family that takes in all shapes and sizes,
including the Rock Shag, Pygmy Cormorant,
and Imperial Shag, as well as the Flightless
Cormorant of the Galápagos Islands. So just
about wherever you go in the world, you will
see one of nature's finest piscators at work.

Gannet
Morus bassanus

Or, should I say, the Northern Gannet to give him
his appropriate name, as I have only just realized
that the Gannets with whom I spent time in
Australia and New Zealand are actually different
birds to the British coastal Gannets. Although
they look practically the same, the Northerner is
bigger and found all over North Africa, Europe,
Greenland, Canada, and North America, while the
Australasian Gannet is only in Australia and New
Zealand. Both are sleek and graphic types like
aerodynamic time-trialing cyclists and are expert
plunge divers who hunt in packs. The birds glide
over the water, eyeing their prey, then descend
together, beaks first, like a cargo of bayonets
falling out of a helicopter. Escape is doubtful and
their successful fishing technique has garnered
them a bad reputation of being a greedy guts. It's
also a well-deserved nickname for those of us who,
from time to time, have eyeballs bigger than our
bellies and like to eat like Gannets.

Magellanic and Galápagos Penguin
Spheniscus magellanicus and *Spheniscus mendiculus*

The Magellanic Penguin looks very much akin to the Galápagos Penguin apart from two details: an extra horseshoe band on his breast and being a much bigger and bulkier bird, more in keeping with the Humboldt. Each Magellanic Penguin's speckled marking is particular to the bird and as unique as a snowflake. The Galápagos Penguin, meanwhile, is unique in itself, as it is the only penguin that lives in the northern hemisphere. (Though only by 62 miles north.) The Galápagos Islands are home to many extraordinary and rare reptiles, mammals, birds, and flora, and this penguin is one of them. Alongside many of the endemic creatures, the penguins are endangered and are very much at risk of extinction. Humans inhabiting the islands have brought their own threats with pollution and pets, but it is the equatorial heat that can wipe out huge numbers, with El Niño heating the water, displacing currents, and destabilizing food chains, starving the ocean of nutrients and starving our penguins alike.

Little Penguin
Eudyptula minor

Our smallest penguin, who is no bigger than a jackdaw in a wetsuit, is a big hit Down Under. Known locally as Fairy Blues and Kororãs in New Zealand, this little ripper nests in burrows across great swathes of bushy coastline and predator-free islands off southern Australia and the whole of New Zealand. Size aside, these metallic-blue ankle-biters are still very able seamen and spend the whole day at sea catching anchovies, sprats, and arrow squid. They wait until dusk to make a moonlit scramble across the beach to their nesting holes in small floundering parties, using the cover of darkness to stumble home out of sight of potential predators, unbeknownst to the fact they are bumbling past a grandstand of joyous tourists who are there just to see the cutest penguins in the world.

Blue-footed Booby
Sula nebouxii

Probably the most popularly named bird in this book, the Blue-footed Booby's name will no doubt get a few chortles from those of you who find that kind of thing funny. All the boobies, including the stunning Nazca Booby and the abundant Brown Booby, are very closely related to Gannets and take up their patch along the equator and further south. Our Blue-footed friends are resident on the west coast of the Americas, from Mexico down to Chile, including the Galápagos. Like their kinsmen, boobies are voracious, nose-diving predators that descend in unison on shoals of fish and are every bit as exacting and imposing as the Gannets at sea. But it is on dry land where they attain their name, as the males like to flap their heavenly, sky-blue feet during courtship, like a clumsy first-time flipper-wearer struggling to walk to the water. This ungainliness got them the "booby" in their name, as *bobo* is Spanish for "stupid" and "clown." I'm not sure the sardines and mackerel are laughing when the last thing they see is this torpedo plummeting toward them, though …

Australian Pelican
Pelecanus conspicillatus

Pelicans are eons old: fossils have been found from 30 million years ago matching with present-day species pretty much exactly, from their loose-necked fishing pouch to their titanic wingspan. There are eight kinds of pelicans, including the American White, Brown, and Peruvian of the Americas. There's the Pink-Backed and Great White of Africa and the Spotted-billed and Dalmatian Pelicans of Eurasia ... Which leaves this guy, my favorite, the Australian Pelican. I just love the way he swaggers along the beach like he owns it, like a steroid freak in a Speedo, arguing and bantering with his fellow Aussie Pelicans before he splashes into the water in ungainly fashion, like a clumsy dog, and then gracefully glides away like a swan.

Magnificent Frigatebird
Fregata magnificens

This amazing seabird of the Gulf of Mexico,
Caribbean Sea, and South Atlantic Ocean
derives its name from the fast and dangerous
three-masted, fully rigged warships that it
resembled in times of yore—and also because
it really is magnificent. Like many seabirds,
Magnificent Frigatebirds have a primordial
look, with long-bladed wings like a pterodactyl,
roaming the coastline on a Caribbean holiday.
A more familiar shape and forked silhouette to
liken it to would be a red kite with an airbag.
The bulbous red puffed-up pouch is not like
that of a pelican for storing fish, but instead
it is a gular sac of stark contrasting red and
black, designed for one purpose only: attracting
ladies. Whoever has the biggest, brightest,
bounciest bird bag gets the chicks!

Black Skimmer
Rynchops niger

It looks like a tern with a terrible case of jaw jut—a real ugly duckling—but the Black Skimmer is actually a remarkable catch. For his colossal underbite is not just for bragging rights in the breeding ground nor for spellbinding the dames. No, as the Black Skimmer flies gracefully with his long wings on slow beats over the warm waters he inhabits, his lower jaw is dropped into the water and dragged along, just skimming the surface … and when contact is made with a fish, the jaw is quickly snapped shut and the skimmer is up and away to enjoy his catch. The Black Skimmer of the Americas is the most sustainable trawler fisherman ever to have graced the seas.

Yellow-eyed Penguin
Megadyptes antipodes

The truth is, there are really not that many really unique kinds of penguin. On the whole, they can be classified into five categories. First you have the Great Penguins—the Emperor and the King. Then there are the Banded Penguins—Humboldt, Magellanic and so on. There are the Crested—the dudes with the blond locks. The Brush-tailed includes the Gentoo and cousins. And, finally, there are the Little Penguins—blue and white. And then there's this guy, who is a species all on his own: the Megadyptes. The Yellow-eyed Penguin's bloodline runs back in time unchanged for 15 million years. Like the Hoatzin, Sandhill Crane, and Ibis, he is one of the most ancient birds alive today. Residing along the southern shores of New Zealand and on nearby islands, this amazing bird, known locally as Hoiho, is a top spot for anybody in the world as he returns home to the shoreline from a nautical day's hunting—ready to stand, motionless, warming his sea-cold bones in the descending brightness of the day, squinting with the sun in his eyes.

Surf Scoter
Melanitta perspicillata

A sea duck of cold water, the Surf Scoter breeds inland in North America and Canada, up in the Great Lakes beside boreal forests and snow perma-peaked mountains. But come winter the suitcase is packed and the Surf Scoters head south and hit the beach. It's not exactly the beach—more like the spindrift and spume of river mouths, estuaries, and shallow bays—but the birds come prepared anyway in a black wetsuit and with a colorful hefty beak, which looks like it was designed and shaped by an old Californian surfer on Venice Beach: perfect for carving the choppy surf in the rough water they ply. Hang ten, dudes, hope it's not too gnarly!

Osprey
Pandion haliaetus

Ah, the magnificent migrating seahawk, whose
arrival in the UK and North America after
wintering in Africa and South America is heralded
with yelps and party poppers exploding from inside
the hides and from behind the camera screens set
up around the handful of Osprey nesting sites.
Rightly so, too, as they are magnificent birds:
large, buzzard-size, black-and-white raptors
with short buzz-cut crests that send tourists and
birders in a tizzy during spring and summer. From
the headlines and attractions it's hard to imagine
that the Osprey is in fact one of the world's most
widely distributed birds, living everywhere except
the Antarctic; it has adapted to almost any kind of
watery terrain. From UK lochs and rivers to the
sandy seaboard of Australia, the Osprey will swoop
and hook his catch of gray mullet, bream, salmon,
and even pike with dexterous ease into the air,
lugging it away without even getting his feet wet.

White-tailed Sea Eagle
Haliaeetus albicilla

The mighty, dreadnaught Sea Eagle of Eurasia was once commonplace on the UK's northern rocky shores, but it was sadly persecuted zealously for fear of losing livestock. They finally became extinct in Great Britain in the very early 1900s. The bird is huge, with a brilliant white tail like a cutter's sail, the wingspan of a tanker, the cruel bite of a great white, and talons that, once they have sunk deep into you, are as immovable as an anchor. With these formidable weapons and an expansive large hunting ground, the Sea Eagles soar and ponder merely whether it'll be freshwater or saltwater fish for supper. A close relative of the American Bald Eagle in many ways, but without the striking, emblematic white head, White-tailed Sea Eagles live all the way from Scandinavia, across Russia, and into Japan, not setting foot in the Bald Eagle's US territory. From the 1970s onward, through careful management, White-tailed Sea Eagles were reintroduced to the west coast of Scotland and have successfully bred and now taken the isles of Mull and Skye as home, with great news of them spreading east. I feel Scotland is an appropriate birthplace; they will be looked after there. In Gaelic they were known as "iolar súil na gréine," which means "The Eagle with the Sunlit Eye." I love that.

White-flippered Penguin
Eudyptula minor albosignata

The White-flippered Penguin is generally considered among scientists to be just a color morph of the Little Penguin and therefore a subspecies, but actually it is a touch bigger and a completely different color. You can see from this book that there isn't always a lot to differentiate between most of the breeds in the penguin world, so a variety in size and color makes a pretty good argument to be a separate species to me. These guys are more of a stonewash blue compared to the Little Penguin's indigo denim, and they're a jay compared to the Little's jackdaw by only a half inch or so. What is the big difference, though, is not just the white dorsal flipper markings but a characteristic that diversifies these dudes from every other penguin species: they are night owls, spending all day hanging out in their colonies and only heading for their fish supper once the sun has set.

Gyrfalcon
Falco rusticolus

What's a bird like you doing in a book like this?
The largest of the falcon family, the Gyrfalcon
is bigger than some of our buzzards, but cleaner
cut and stark in his winter freckle-pied plumage.
The Gyrfalcon is a native of the cold north,
located in North America, Canada, Greenland,
and northern Europe. The circled path of the
Gyrfalcon commonly leads its way above the
tundra and mountains of its fatherland, but
when winter peaks and food is scarce, the
Viking's prize is a secret seabird. Recent research
has revealed that they spend the dim days of
midwinter coursing the ice floes and icebergs for
new prey, switching their diet from lapwings and
lemmings to gulls and guillemots, who have left
their colonies post-breeding to spend their days
at sea. Whole seasons are spent on the packed ice
and glacial masses that float offshore and become
a temporary biosphere for our hardiest falcon.

SPOTTING AND JOTTING

It's great spotting a seabird you've never seen before. Even if some of these birds fly (or swim!) a little further afield, you'd be surprised at how many you might be lucky enough to spot. So here's a handy way of keeping all your jottings in check. Get spotting either sitting comfortably at your window or pack your boots and binoculars and go on your travels across the globe. Happy spotting!

☐ Emperor Penguin

☐ King Penguin

☐ Brown Skua

☐ Wandering Albatross

☐ Storm Petrel

☐ Sooty Shearwater

☐ Northern Giant Petrel

☐ Gentoo Penguin

☐ Adélie Penguin

☐ Striated Caracara

☐ Snowy Sheathbill

☐ Imperial Shag

☐ Arctic Tern

117

☐ Chinstrap Penguin

☐ Common Loon

☐ Northern Fulmar

☐ Northern and Southern
Rockhopper Penguin

☐ Parasitic Jaeger

☐ Steller's Eider

☐ Macaroni Penguin

☐ King Eider

☐ Royal Penguin

☐ Harlequin Duck

☐ Smew

☐ Crested Auklet

120

☐ Dovekie

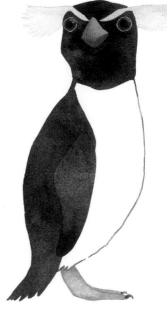

☐ Fiordland Crested Penguin and
  Snares Penguin

☐ Erect-crested Penguin

☐ Great Auk

☐ Puffin

☐ Razorbill

☐ Guillemot

122

□ Humboldt Penguin

□ African Penguin

□ Tufted Puffin

123

☐ Rhinoceros Auklet

☐ Gannet

☐ Great
Cormorant

☐ Magellanic and Galápagos Penguin

☐ Little Penguin

☐ Australian Pelican

☐ Blue-footed Booby

125

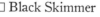 □ Black Skimmer

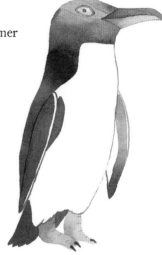

□ Yellow-eyed Penguin

□ Magnificent Frigatebird

□ Surf Scoter

☐ Osprey

☐ White-tailed Sea Eagle

☐ Gyrfalcon

☐ White-flippered Penguin

127

ACKNOWLEDGMENTS

Thank yous:

To my goldfinches, Jess, Romy, and Mae. To the
Sewells, the Lees, and the Roses.

To Megan Lee, all at Caught By The River,
Simon Benham, the Free University of Glastonbury
and The Crow's Nest, Richard King and the
Green Man, JK, the Montague Place Street Team,
and all the friendly folk of the Shire.

Massive shout-out to all the seabird
conservationists: keep up the good fight!